I0393807

Table of contents

1. Agency identifying information

TABLE 1:   AGENCY IDENTIFYING INFORMATION

Part A	
1. Agency	Consumer Financial Protection Bureau
2. Address	1700 G Street NW
3. City, State, Zip code	Washington, DC 20552
4. CPDF Code	FR FT
5. FIPS code	110001, 06075, 176031, 36061

2. Total employment

TABLE 2: TOTAL EMPLOYMENT

Part B	
Permanent full-time and part-time employees	960
Temporary employees	383
Employees paid from non-appropriated funds	0
TOTAL EMPLOYMENT	1343

3. Leadership

TABLE 3: LEADERSHIP

Part C	
Head of agency	Richard Cordray Director, Financial Protection Bureau
Agency Head Designee	M. Stacey Bach Director, Equal Employment Opportunity
Principal EEO Director/Official	N/A
Title VII Affirative EEO Program Official	N/A
Section 501 Affirmative Action Program Official	N/A
Complaint Processing Program Manager	N/A
Other Responsible EEO Staff	Donald D. Pettaway Senior Equal Employment Opportunity Specialist

4. List of subordinate components covered in this report

FIGURE 1: CFPB SUPERVISION REGIONS

CFPB Supervision regions

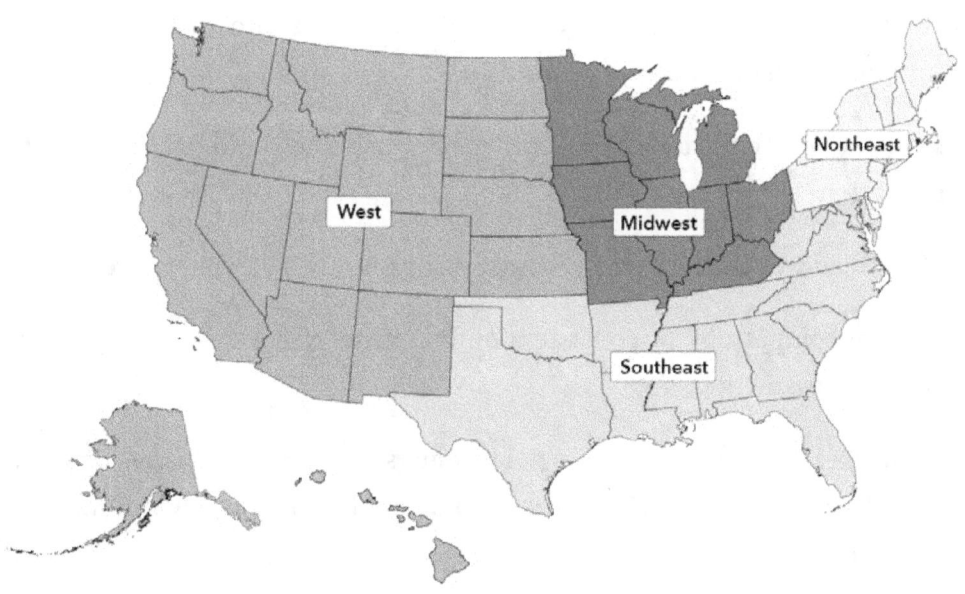

Regions

- Northeast

- Southeast

- Midwest

- West

5. Executive summary

The Consumer Financial Protection Bureau (CFPB or Bureau) is the nation's first federal agency focused solely on consumer financial protection. The Dodd-Frank Wall Street Reform and Consumer Protection Act (Pub. L. 111-203) (July 21, 2010) (Dodd-Frank Act) created the CFPB to protect consumers and to encourage fair and competitive consumer financial markets.

The Bureau's mission is to make consumer financial markets work for American consumers, honest businesses, and the economy as a whole. The Dodd-Frank Act requires the CFPB to:

- Ensure that consumers have timely and understandable information to make responsible decisions about financial transactions;

- Protect consumers from unfair, deceptive, or abusive acts and practices, and from discrimination;

- Identify and address outdated, unnecessary, or unduly burdensome regulations;

- Promote fair competition by consistent enforcement of the consumer protection laws in the Bureau's jurisdiction; and

- Ensure markets for consumer financial products and services operate transparently and efficiently to facilitate access and innovation. (*See* Dodd-Frank Act, Pub. L. No. 111-203, Sec. 1021(b)).

The CFPB began operations approximately three years ago on July 21, 2011. The Bureau works to educate consumers, enforce consumer financial laws, and study available information to better understand consumers, financial services providers, and consumer financial markets. To accomplish these goals, the CFPB is divided into six Divisions:

- Consumer Education & Engagement (CEE)

- Supervision, Fair Lending & Enforcement (SEFL)

- Research, Markets & Regulations (RMR)

- External Affairs (EA)

- Legal (LD)

- Operations (OPS)

These Divisions work together to:

- Write rules, supervise regulated entities, and enforce federal consumer financial protection laws;

- Restrict unfair, deceptive, or abusive acts or practices;

- Take consumer complaints;

- Promote financial education;

- Research consumer behavior;

- Monitor financial markets for new risks to consumers; and

- Enforce laws that outlaw discrimination and other unfair treatment in consumer finance.

This Equal Employment Opportunity (EEO) Program Status Report for Fiscal Year (FY) 2013 highlights CFPB's accomplishments in FY13 in establishing a model EEO Program and identifies areas where the Bureau will take further actions to improve its EEO Program.

Ensuring the rights of all CFPB employees and applicants for employment with CFPB are protected from unlawful discrimination is achieved through the partnerships of the Office of Equal Employment Opportunity (EEO Office), the Office of Minority and Women Inclusion (OMWI), and the Office of Human Capital (OHC). Pursuant to Section 342 of the Dodd-Frank Act, OMWI develops standards for equal employment opportunity and diversity, the OHC incorporates those standards into CFPB Human Capital Management, and the offices of EEO, OMWI, and OHC monitor the impacts and results, cultivate successful policies and practices, and develop mitigating strategies to strengthen all EEO and diversity programs. These collaborations support CFPB's mission by ensuring fairness and equality under the law for all employees and applicants for employment and by cultivating a working environment that supports staff in their efforts to protect consumers.

5.1   Essential element 1: demonstrated commitment from CFPB leadership

Since its inception, the Bureau has been committed to maintaining a workplace that promotes professionalism and productivity and an environment that respects the dignity of all, and embraces transparency and education of employees about their EEO rights and responsibilities. When possible equal opportunity issues have been identified, the Bureau has immediately committed to diagnosing issues and taking appropriate corrective action when warranted.

In February 2013, Director Richard Cordray reaffirmed the Bureau's commitment to EEO through an email to all employees containing his EEO policy statement. Director Cordray's policy statement is readily available to all employees on the EEO page of the CFPB's intranet. The information contained in the Director's statement is also available on the CFPB's public website. Further, monthly and jointly, Director Cordray meets with leadership from OHC, OMWI, EEO, EA and the Strategy Office to discuss the CFPB initiatives that support goals to recruit broadly and strategically. One initiative enlisted senior leadership to host outreach events to attract people to CFPB as a "best place to serve."

Additionally, posters, training, and other information are available on the intranet and are issued through all-employee email distributions from the Director and the Chief Operating Officer (COO) to educate employees about the EEO program and the anti-discrimination and anti-retaliation protections available to federal employees. EEO information is also provided to supervisors and managers directly through OHC's "Manager Minute" publication.

Information about how to file an EEO complaint is distributed to all new employees during orientation and is readily available on the intranet and internet; the EEO Office has an email account and a toll-free telephone number to accommodate those wishing to file a complaint without coming into the EEO Office.

Leadership is also committed to resolving workplace conflicts. To this end, CFPB has imposed a mandatory requirement that all managers participate in alternative dispute resolution (ADR) if elected by an employee, absent extenuating circumstances.

Leadership is also committed to constant improvement in the areas of employee engagement and morale. For example, CFPB Leadership supports a deeper analysis of the Annual Employee Survey (AES) to analyze differences in perception among demographic groups. In FY13, OMWI examined employee feedback to gain insight into CFPB's organizational culture through a set of twenty survey items to measure employee perception as it relates to workplace inclusion in the categories of: Fair, Open, Cooperative, Supportive and Empowered. Derived from an 81 percent participation rate for the survey, these twenty had the highest positive correlation to the formation and sustainment of an inclusive workplace.

Finally, the CFPB plans to launch a formal mentorship program to help employees navigate the CFPB culture, build relationships, and leverage opportunities. Additional plans include OMWI leading the development of an executive diversity council to increase cross-divisional collaboration for diversity initiatives through the support of key leaders at the Bureau, which is scheduled to launch in April 2014.

5.2 Essential element 2: integration of EEO into the CFPB's strategic mission

The newly established EEO Office is working to ensure that EEO is an everyday part of the Bureau's business and guides its strategic goals.

The CFPB has developed a Strategic Plan for FY13 through FY15, and CFPB Strategic Goal 4 is to advance CFPB's performance by maximizing resource productivity and enhancing impact; building on this goal, the Office of Human Capital's strategic plan includes the following strategy:

Strategy 4.1.1: Recruitment, Engagement, and Total Rewards - Recruit and retain a high-quality, diverse staff through effective workforce planning and talent acquisition methods, strong engagement, diversity, and inclusion programs, and a competitive total rewards package.

The EEO Office will also work toward including as a strategic goal in subsequent years attaining and maintaining Model EEO Program status by incorporating the Six Essential Elements identified by the EEOC.

Currently, each supervisor and manager's performance plan at the Bureau includes criteria seeking an assessment of their ability to grow and retain a diverse staff and on the competencies of collaboration, communication, problem-solving, and adaptability. In addition to working to incorporate EEO into the strategic goals of CFPB, the new EEO Office has visibility into the organization because it is administratively housed in the Operations Division where the team can work closely with fellow colleagues in OHC and OMWI and learn about new programs, policies, and initiatives during their development phase.

Leadership's commitment is further demonstrated by the support, development and implementation of a comprehensive workforce planning process that aligns with the annual budget process. OHC developed a Workforce Planning Handbook and completed the implementation of a new position management and position-approval process. These tools allow for greater visibility into planned positions and can be used to ensure a consistent approach to diversity recruitment, focus Bureau resources on critical hires, and provide oversight of any organizational change efforts.

CFPB designated an Acting Director for the EEO Office beginning in February 2013. The work of the Acting Director and assistance provided by detailees and contractors in FY13 provided a preliminary structure for the EEO program, and the Acting Director began building on existing relationships to cultivate the dynamic partnerships required for integration of EEO into CFPB's strategic mission. The permanent appointment of the Acting Director in December 2013 and staffing of the EEO Office to date will help start to establish the permanence and support necessary to identify and provide counsel on appropriate linkages of EEO goals to the goals supporting the CFPB Mission and Strategic Goals, OHC strategic goals, OMWI goals, and further EEO accountability for the Bureau. The Bureau is assessing the resource needs necessary to establish a robust program, and the EEO Office intends to work toward achieving full capacity.

Pursuant to a request from the EEO Office and OMWI, FY13 marks the first year CFPB had complete applicant flow data to be used for the identification of triggers and possible barriers within the Bureau's selection process, and OMWI and OHC in conjunction with the EEO Office have begun preliminary assessments of the data.

As the EEO Office matures, a better assessment of the necessary competencies and resources required for conducting the MD-715 analyses, managing Special Emphasis and Affirmative Employment Programs for the Bureau, implementing the 29 C.F.R. Part 1614 complaint-processing procedures, monitoring CFPB's external-facing civil rights law compliance, providing on-going training opportunities, and ensuring the EEO program is effectively implemented will be able to be conducted. Workforce planning is underway.

5.3 Essential element 3: management and program accountability

During FY13, the Bureau did not discipline any employees for discrimination, retaliation, harassment, or an infraction of any provision of law covered by the No FEAR Act or 29 C.F.R. Part 1614. This is consistent with the fact that there were no findings of discrimination by Final Agency Decision, by order of the Equal Employment Opportunity Commission (EEOC), the Merit Systems Protection Board, the Office of Special Counsel, or a Federal court, or after a management inquiry conducted by OHC. CFPB did work to ensure prompt compliance with terms of all settlement agreements reached in FY13 and no allegations of non-compliance were filed with the EEO Office in FY13.

The CFPB has hired supervisors and managers from all sectors, including federal government, state and local government, and private industry. Upon arrival at CFPB in FY13, all new employees attend "New Employee Orientation." This is a 3-day course that includes collaboration and communication training.

All employees are also required to complete annual No FEAR Act and harassment prevention training. CFPB completion rate for No FEAR Act training was 93% during FY13. A two-year program requiring all supervisors and managers attend 40 hours of basic supervisory training was also launched, and 75% of managers were slated to complete courses by the end of December 2013. This training addresses, among other human capital areas, EEO in the workplace.

The EEO Office arranged in FY13 for legal counsel from the EEOC to provide a two-hour, on-site EEO overview session to managers and supervisors (May 22, 2013), for the EEOC Training Institute to conduct two 8-hour EEO overviews for supervisors and managers (June 12 & 19, 2013), for a disability law expert from the Department of Justice to provide on-site training regarding disability law (June 13, 2013), and for the Director of the Americans with Disabilities Act (ADA) and Equal Employment Opportunity (EEO) Services section of the National Employment Law Institute (NELI) to provide half day training to OHC, LD, and supervisors and managers about addressing ADA-related human resource workplace situations and questions (July 24, 2013). The EEO Office also arranged for the NELI training to be provided to 140 Supervision, Enforcement and Fair Lending (SEFL) supervisors and managers at SEFL's 2nd Quarter Manager Training Seminar (January 13, 2014). Diversity and inclusion training with Laura Liswood, hosted by OMWI, was also conducted on various dates in FY13 for all employees in an effort to expand awareness, knowledge, and cultural competencies that aid in the understanding and management of a diverse workforce and its values to the CFPB mission.

Attendees rated these presentations highly, which the EEO Office anticipates may help it obtain institutional support for an expanded EEO and diversity training curriculum. Additional training on an initial and refresher basis will be provided as the EEO Office grows.

As a new agency, CFPB is still in the process of developing policies and procedures and its training and promotion systems; resources permitting, the EEO office intends to work hand-in-hand with program offices as policies, programs, and procedures are developed and periodically reviewed and will have a particular focus on working with other stakeholders related to review. The EEO Office will also foster a collaborative relationship with other stakeholders across the Bureau to ensure effective coordination with related human capital and management programs.

The Bureau promotes early resolution of complaints and the use of alternative dispute resolution (ADR) as an option to its traditional administrative EEO complaint processes and offers ADR at all stages of the EEO complaint process. The commitment to ADR is communicated to employees through the intranet, training, and during individual meetings with parties seeking assistance from the EEO Office. During FY13, the Bureau mediated three or 33 percent of its nine formal complaints and resolution was reached in all. The Bureau also offers ADR to persons through OHC when non-EEO workplace conflicts are raised. ADR offered through the EEO Office or through OHC is conducted by qualified ADR professionals with whom the Bureau contracts to ensure neutrality and to foster trust of participants.

Finally, the EEO Office has worked closely with representatives from Technology and Innovation (TI), Consumer Education and Engagement (CEE), and OHC to establish a new position where the incumbent will collaborate with program officials at all levels throughout CFPB to determine and ensure compliance with the Rehabilitation Act regarding accessibility for employees and members of the public. Specifically, once onboard, the employee will evaluate and improve upon the accessibility of CFPB information and technology products and services in accordance with the Rehabilitation Act and CFPB policies, program goals and objectives. A cross-divisional disability working group spearheaded by the EEO Office worked on other projects including enhancements to raise visibility of the option of using Schedule A appointments to on-board qualified persons with disabilities, the dissemination of disability etiquette, and raising awareness about ensuring equal access.

5.4   Essential element 4: proactive prevention of unlawful discrimination

CFPB is committed to preventing prohibited conduct before it occurs. The EEO Office offers forward-facing assistance, including formal and informal training opportunities and day-to-day assistance through its Open Door policy. Managers are encouraged to consult early and often with the EEO Office to learn about how to comply with EEO obligations. Expanded resources will enable the EEO Office to provide additional proactive assistance to prevent unlawful discrimination, harassment, and retaliation. The level of proactive support that will be offered in future fiscal years will correlate directly with resources available to the EEO Office that are not dedicated to complaint processing.

The EEO Office has made significant progress in providing all employees with information to orient them to their rights and responsibilities under the various anti-discrimination and anti-retaliation laws that apply in the federal sector through posters, intranet content, all-employee emails, and policy statements from the Director. Targeted guidance for managers has also been provided, including sending a copy of the Director's policy statement and intranet resources to each newly on-boarded or promoted supervisor or manager.

The EEO Office has made a good faith effort to collect, analyze, and identify potential barriers to equal employment opportunity at CFPB. Because the office opened in February 2013, however, it has not yet been able to conduct further inquiry into all relevant circumstances about whether an actual barrier exists and the various factors contributing to creation of any identified barriers. The EEO Office will continue to dedicate time and resources to this important project and to collaborate with OHC and OMWI to assess relevant policies, procedures, and practices; review workforce data and trends, review complaints, surveys, feedback from exit interviews and focus groups, and research literature; and assess whether any barriers are job-related and consistent with business necessity. Once the EEO Office has this comprehensive picture, it will be in a better position to develop strategic plans to eliminate identified barriers. The EEO Office is also committed to conducting a self-assessment on an annual basis as set forth in this Report and intends to monitor progress, potential barriers, and identified barriers more frequently than on an annual basis when resources exist for doing so.

Following review by the EEOC in accordance with Executive Order 13164, CFPB released a comprehensive Reasonable Accommodation policy and program for its employees in July 2013. Since that time, the reasonable accommodations program has continued to mature. Requests for reasonable accommodation are processed through the Employee and Labor Relations Team in OHC, and all were timely completed in FY13.

5.5 Essential element 5: efficiency

CFPB's EEO Program is committed to achieving model status by virtue of the Bureau's complaints processing, alternative dispute resolution (ADR) program, training, data collection, tracking, and assessment. CFPB is a data-driven, 21st century agency that embraces the use of technology to meet mission needs.

Since its inception, CFPB has provided a fair and efficient dispute resolution system in accordance with 29 C.F.R. Part 1614, first by contracting with the United States Department of Treasury in FY11 and FY12 for EEO complaint-processing services, and second by offering EEO complaint-processing at CFPB conducted through qualified third-party contractors from the GSA Schedule for counseling, mediation, and investigation services in FY13 and beyond. CFPB's goal for future fiscal years is to have an average of 180 days or less in complaints investigation (absent allowable extensions), in line with the regulatory requirements.

With respect to the reasonable accommodation program, the CFPB has completed 25 reasonable accommodation requests and 100% of the requested were completed timely; OHC is committed to meeting all processing timeframes again in FY14 and beyond. Importantly, the Bureau has a central funding mechanism in place for processing reasonable accommodation requests to ensure that ample monetary resources exist for complying with legal obligations.

The EEO Office finalized an ADR policy in Q3 of FY13, further underscoring CFPB's commitment to ADR. The widespread use of ADR is encouraged to help resolve workplace disputes in the earliest possible stages. This is handled through both the EEO process and OHC for non-EEO workplace disputes, and supervisors and managers must participate in ADR when requested to do so by the EEO Office or OHC. Through this program, the Bureau has achieved success in gaining resolution for workplace disputes.

Tracking systems related to EEO matters need some improvement for the EEO program to work at maximum efficiency. Although OHC has an effective means to track whether and when required and optional EEO training has been taken, other tracking systems are not yet in place. To date, the EEO Office does not have access to a complaint-tracking software system to help ensure timely, accurate data for both monitoring and reporting purposes. This software has been requested and the EEO Office's goal is to obtain it as soon as possible. OHC has similarly requested software that will be used to increase efficiency of its reasonable accommodation program.

5.6 Essential element 6: responsiveness and legal compliance

CFPB is committed to ensuring full compliance with the law and incorporating EEO best practices into its everyday business. As a new agency, the CFPB has the opportunity to develop each of its policies and programs and has thoughtfully aimed to ensure that each new policy and program abides by all applicable legal requirements and incorporates best practices. When possible issues have become apparent through self-monitoring, CFPB leadership has committed to diagnosing issues and making any necessary adjustments to ensure that CFPB's commitment to equality and fairness is lived daily.

There have been no findings of discrimination imposed against CFPB to date. In addition, no EEOC order imposing corrective action has been implemented. Timely submissions from the Bureau have been provided for the Form 462 Report, the Federal Equal Opportunity Recruitment Program (FEORP) Report, the Disabled Veterans Affirmative Action Program (DVAAP) Report, and annual No FEAR Act Report, and the MD-715 Report.

In FY 2013, 93% of employees completed the No FEAR Act Training, and 92% of employees completed sexual harassment prevention training. The EEO Office will collaborate with OHC to work to achieve higher completion rates in FY14 and beyond.

6. Workforce analysis

TABLE 4: TOTAL WORKFORCE – FY 2012

	ALL	Hispanic	White	Black	Asian	NH/OPI	AI/AN	Two or More
ALL	988	46	653	176	93	2	9	9
%		4.65%	66.09%	17.81%	9.41%	0.20%	0.91%	0.91%
CLF		5.44%	72.36%	12.02%	3.90%	0.14%	1.08%	0.54%
Male	497	20	357	66	45	1	5	3
Female	491	26	296	110	48	1	4	6

TABLE 5: TOTAL WORKFORCE – FY 2013

	ALL	Hispanic	White	Black	Asian	NH/OPI	AI/AN	Two or More
ALL	1,343	73	888	228	131	2	9	12
%		5.44%	66.12%	16.98%	9.76%	0.14%	0.67%	0.89%
CLF		5.44%	72.36%	12.02%	3.90%	0.14%	1.08%	0.54%
Male	715	37	508	91	69	1	6	3
Female	628	36	380	137	62	1	3	9

TABLE 6: TOTAL WORKFORCE – FY 2012 COMPARED TO FY 2013

	ALL	Hispanic	White	Black	Asian	NH/OPI	AI/AN	Two or More
Difference	+355	+27	+235	+52	+38	0	0	+3
Male	+218	+17	+151	+25	+24	0	+1	0
Female	+137	+10	+84	+27	+14	0	-1	+3
Ratio Change	0.00%							
Male	2.94%	0.73%	1.69%	0.10%	0.58%	-0.03%	-0.06%	-0.08%
Female	-2.94%	0.05%	-1.66%	-0.93%	-0.24%	-0.03%	-0.18%	0.06%
Net Change	35.93%							
Male	43.86%	85.00%	42.30%	37.88%	53.33%	0.00%	20.00%	0.00%
Female	27.90%	38.46%	28.38%	24.55%	29.17%	0.00%	-25.0%	50.00%

At the close of FY13, CFPB employed a total of 1,343 employees—960 permanent employees and 383 temporary employees. This was a significant increase of 264 permanent employees (37.93%) and 91 (31.16%) temporary employees for a net increase of 355 employees compared to FY12.

Males comprised 715 or 53.24% of the permanent workforce—slightly higher when compared to the 2010 national civilian labor force (CLF) availability of 51.86%. Females comprised 628 or 46.76% of the permanent workforce as compared to 48.14% of the CLF.

6.1   Permanent workforce: participation of class grouping

TABLE 7:   WORKFORCE (ALL)

Group	Total No. FY 2013	Percentage	FY12 No.	Percentage	Net Change	CLF
White Male	508	37.83%	357	36.13%	42.30%	38.33%
White Female	380	28.29%	296	29.96%	28.38%	34.30%
Black Male	91	6.70%	66	6.68%	37.88%	5.49%
Black Female	137	10.20%	110	11.13%	24.55%	6.53%
Hispanic Male	37	2.76%	20	2.02%	85.00%	5.17%
Hispanic Female	36	2.68%	26	2.63%	38.46%	4.79%
Asian Male	69	5.14%	45	4.55%	53.33%	1.97%
Asian Female	62	4.62%	48	4.86%	29.17%	1.93%
NH/PI Male	1	0.70%	1	0.10%	0.00%	0.07%
NH/PI Female	1	0.70%	1	0.10%	0.00%	0.07%
AI/AN Male	6	0.45%	5	0.51%	20.00%	0.55%
AI/AN Male	3	0.22%	4	0.40%	-25.00%	0.53%
2 or More Male	3	0.22%	3	0.30%	0.00%	0.26%
2 or More Female	9	0.67%	6	0.61%	50.00%	0.28%

White females are employed at CFPB at a rate of 28.29% (380), which is below the CLF of 34.30%. Hispanic males appear at a rate of 2.76% (37) and Hispanic females at 2.68% (36), which are significantly below the CLF of 5.17% and 4.79%, respectively. American Indian/Alaska Native males are employed at 0.45% (06) and females at 0.22% (03), which were below the CLF availability of 0.55% and 0.53%, respectively. Males who are two or More Races were reported at 0.22% (03)—slightly below the CLF of 0.26%.

Asian males are employed at a rate of 5.14% (69) and Asian females at 4.62% (62), which were significantly above the CLF of 1.97% and 1.93% respectively. Black males were employed by CFPB at a rate of 6.70% (91) and females at 10.20% (137), which were above the CLF of 5.49% and 6.53%, respectively. Females who are two or More Races were employed at 0.67% (9), which is above the CLF of 0.28%. All other groups are at or above the CLF for their group.

6.2   Temporary workforce: participation of class grouping

TABLE 8:   TEMPORARY WORKFORCE

Group	Total No. FY 2013	Percentage	FY12 No.	Percentage	Net Change
White Male	154	40%	104	35.62%	48.08%
White Female	107	27.94%	86	29.45%	24.42%
Black Male	20	5.22%	17	5.82%	17.65%
Black Female	32	8.36%	28	9.59%	14.29%
Hispanic Male	9	2.35%	5	1.71%	80.00%
Hispanic Female	10	2.61%	10	3.42%	0.00%
Asian Male	26	6.79%	18	6.16%	44.44%
Asian Female	20	5.22%	22	7.53%	0.00%
NH/PI Male	0	0.00%	0	0.00%	0.00%
NH/PI Female	0	0.00%	0	0.00%	0.00%

AI/AN Male	0	0.00%	0	0.00%	0.00%
AI/AN Male	0	0.00%	0	0.00%	0.00%
2 or More Male	2	0.52%	1	0.34%	100%
2 or More Female	3	0.78%	1	0.34%	200%

At the end of FY13 there were no Native Hawaiian/Pacific Islanders males or females and no American Indian/Alaskan Natives males or females in the temporary workforce. With the exception of Asian females, with a decrease of -2%, all other groups saw net gains in participation rates. Hispanic males net change of 80.00% (from 5 to 9 employees) and males and females who are Two or More Races were the highest net changes areas for CFPB. Hispanic females remained unchanged.

6.3 Analysis of senior pay bands by grouping (permanent employees)

White males and females are represented in all of the senior grades CN-53 to CN-81/82/90. Black females were represented in all senior grades including CN-81/82/90; however, Black males were not represented at the CN-81/82/90 grade level. Asian males and females are represented in all the senior grades.

Native Hawaiian/Pacific Islanders males are represented at the CN-53 and females are represented at the CN-60. American Indian/Alaskan Native females are represented at the CN-53 level. American Indian/Alaskan Native males are represented at the CN-60 and CN-71 levels. Males and females who are Two or More Races are represented at the CN-53 level and males are represented at the CN-71 grade level.

Hispanic males and females are represented in all the senior grade levels with the exception of the CN81/82/90.

TABLE 9: SENIOR PAY BANDS BY GENDER

	Male	Female
CN53	85	86
	16.87%	18.87%
CN60	100	99
	19.84%	21.71%
CN71	92	84
	18.25%	18.42%
CN81/82/90	17	8
	3.37%	1.75%

EEO Program Status Report for FY 2013

TABLE 10: SENIOR PAY BANDS BY GROUPING

	W/M	WF	BM	BF	HM	HF	AM	AF	NH/PI M	NH/PI F	AI/AN M	AI/AN F	2+M	2+F
CN53	62	53	12	12	5	6	2	14	1	0	2	0	1	1
%	17.5%	19.4%	16.9%	11.4%	17.9%	23.1%	4.7%	33.3%	100%	0.0%	33.3%	0.0%	100%	16.7%
CN60	79	74	11	12	4	4	6	7	0	1	0	1	0	0
	22.3%	27.1%	15.5%	11.4%	14.2%	15.4%	14.0%	16.7%	0.0%	100%	0.1%	16.7%	0.0%	0.0%
CN71	74	63	9	10	3	3	6	4	0	0	0	1	0	3
	20.9%	23.1%	12.7%	9.6%	10.7%	11.5%	14.0%	9.5%	0.0%	0.0%	0.0%	16.7%	0.0%	50.0%
CN81/ 82/ 90	14	6	0	1	0	0	3	1	0	0	0	0	0	0
	3.6%	2.2%	0.0%	1.0%	0.0%	0.0%	7.0%	2.4%	0.0%	0.0%	0.0%	0.0%	0.0%	0.0%

6.4 New hires: permanent

Permanent new hires for FY13 consisted of 124 females (42.32%), which is lower than the CLF availability of 48.14%. White females were 25.26% (74) of the new hires, which is lower than the 34.03% CLF availability. Hispanic females were 3.07% of the new hires, which is lower than the 4.79% CLF availability. Native Hawaiian/Pacific Islanders males and females were not in the permanent hires in FY 2013. American Indian/Alaskan Natives males were .034% of the new hires compared to slightly higher CLF availability of 0.55%. Males and females who are Two or More Races were not in the permanent hires for FY13.

TABLE 11: NEW PERMANENT HIRES BY GENDER

	Male	Female
Number	169	124
Percent	57.68%	42.32%
CLF	51.86%	48.14%

TABLE 12: NEW PERMANENT HIRES BY GROUPING

	WM	WF	BM	BF	HM	HF	AM	AF	NH/PI M	NH/PI F	AI/AN M	AI/AN F	2+M	2+F
#	113	74	20	28	16	9	19	13	0	0	1	0	0	0
%	38.6%	25.2%	6.8%	9.6%	5.5%	3.0%	6.5%	4.4%	0.0%	0.0%	0.3%	0.0%	0.0%	0.0%
CLF	38.3%	34.0%	5.5%	6.5%	5.2%	4.8%	2.0%	1.9%	0.1%	0.1%	0.6%	0.5%	0.3%	0.3%

6.5   New hires: temporary

Temporary hires for FY13 consisted of 61 (28.11%) White females, which is lower than the CLF availability of 34.03%. Black males consisted of (61) or 2.76% of the hires, which is lower than the CLF availability of 5.59%. Hispanic males made up 3.23% (7) of the new hires and Hispanic female consisted of 1.38% (3), which are both lower than the CLF availability of 5.17% and 4.79, respectively. Native Hawaiian/Pacific Islanders males and females and American Indian/Alaska Natives males and females were not in the temporary hires for FY13.

TABLE 13: NEW TEMPORARY HIRES BY GENDER

	Male	Female
Number	128	89
Percent	58.99%	41.01%
CLF	51.86%	48.14%

EEO Program Status Report for FY 2013

TABLE 14: NEW TEMPORARY HIRES BY GENDER

	WM	BM	BF	HM	HF	AM	AF	NH/PI M	NH/PI F	AI/AN M	AI/AN F	2+M	2+F
#	95	6	15	7	3	18	7	0	0	0	0	2	3
%	43.8%	2.8%	6.9%	2.2%	1.4%	8.3%	2.2%	0%	0.0%	0.0%	0.0%	0.9%	1.4%
CLF	38.3%	5.5%	6.5%	5.2%	4.8%	2.0%	1.9%	0.1%	0.1%	0.6%	0.5%	0.3%	0.3%

6.6 New hires by mission critical occupations

CFPB's Strategic Plan identifies four key occupational groups that are instrumental and deemed "mission-critical" to perform the mission of the Bureau.

6.6.1 Economist (0110)

During FY13, CFPB hired 8 Economists (0110 Series), half of which were male and half female:

- 2 or 25.00% were White males

- 2 or 25.00% were White females

- 1 or 12.50% were Black female

- 1 or 12.50% were Hispanic male

- 2 or 12.50% were Asian males

- 2 or 12.50% were Asian females

TABLE 15: NEW ECONOMISTS BY GENDER

	Male	Female
Number	4	4
Percent	50%	50%
CLF	67.10%	32.90%

TABLE 16: NEW ECONOMISTS BY GROUPING

	WM	WF	BM	BF	HM	HF	AM	AF	NH/PI M	NH/PI F	AI/AN M	AI/AN F	2+M	2+F
#	2	2	0	1	1	0	1	1	0	0	0	0	0	0
%	25.0%	25.0%	0.0%	12.5%	12.5%	0.0%	25.0%	25.0%	0.0%	0.0%	0.0%	0.0%	0.0%	0.0%
CLF	56.3%	21.6%	3.2%	2.5%	3.1%	2.0%	5.4%	3.7%	0.0%	0.0%	0.2%	0.1%	1.2%	0.8%

6.6.2 Misc. administration (0301)

During FY13, CFPB hired 91 employees in the Miscellaneous Administration Program (0301 series) occupations, comprised of 53.85% (49) males and 46.15% (42) females:

- White males (31) comprised 34.07% of the hires

- White females (24) comprised 26.37% of the hires

- Black males (5) comprised 5.49% of the hires

- Black females (11) comprised d 12.09% of the hires

- Hispanic males (5) comprised 5.49% of the hires

- Hispanic females (2) comprised 2.20% of the hires

- Asian males (7) comprised 7.69% of the hires

- Asian females (5) comprised 5.59% of the hires

TABLE 17: NEW MISC. ADMINISTRATORS BY GENDER

	Male	Female
Number	49	42
Percent	53.85%	46.15%
CLF	**36.70%**	**63.30%**

EEO Program Status Report for FY 2013

TABLE 18: NEW MISC. ADMINISTRATORS BY GROUPING

	WM	WF	BM	BF	HM	HF	AM	AF	NH/PI M	NH/PI F	AI/AN M	AI/AN F	2+M	2+F
#	31	24	5	11	5	2	7	5	0	0	0	0	1	0
%	34.1%	26.4%	5.5%	12.0%	5.5%	2.2%	7.7%	5.5%	0.0%	0.0%	0.0%	0.0%	1.1%	0.0%
CLF	24.1%	33.8%	7.2%	22.1%	2.6%	2.9%	1.6%	3.0%	0.0%	0.1%	0.2%	0.3%	1.0%	1.1%

6.6.3 Financial institution examining (0570)

A total of 118 Financial Institution Examining (0570 series) employees were hired during FY13, which consisted of 85 or 72.03% males and 33 or 27.97% females:

- White males (56) comprised 47.46% of the hires

- White females (23) comprised 10.49% of the hires

- Black males (11) comprised 9.32% of the hires

- Black females (6) comprised 5.08% of the hires

- Hispanic males (8) comprised 6.78% of the hires

- Hispanic females (2) comprised 1.69% of the hires

- Asian males (1) comprised 8.74% of the hires

- Asian females (2) comprised 1.69% of the hires

TABLE 19: NEW EXAMINERS BY GENDER

	Male	Female
Number	85	33
Percent	72.03%	27.97%
CLF	57.60%	42.40%

EEO Program Status Report for FY 2013

TABLE 20: NEW EXAMINERS BY GROUPING

	WM	WF	BM	BF	HM	HF	AM	AF	NH/PI M	NH/PI F	AI/AN M	AI/AN F	2+M	2+F
#	56	23	11	6	8	2	10	2	0	0	0	0	0	0
%	47.5%	19.5%	9.3%	5.1%	6.9%	1.7%	8.7%	1.7%	0.0%	0.0%	0.0%	0.0%	0.0%	0.0%
CLF	48.3%	30.3%	4.5%	6.9%	2.2%	1.6%	1.9%	2.8%	0.0%	0.0%	0.3%	0.2%	0.4%	0.6%

6.6.4 General attorney (0905)

CFPB hired 78 General Attorneys (0905) during FY13, with an even 50-50 split among men and women at 39 hires each:

- 31 or 39.74% were White males

- 27 or 34.62% were White females

- 2 or 2.50% were Black males

- 6 or 7.69% were Black females

- 1 or 1.28% were Hispanic males

- 2 or 2.56% were Hispanic females

- 5 or 6.41% were Asian males

- 4 or 5.13% were Asian females

TABLE 21: NEW GENERAL ATTORNEYS BY GENDER

	Male	Female
Number	39	39
Percent	50%	50%
CLF	64.90%	35.10%

EEO Program Status Report for FY 2013

TABLE 22: NEW GENERAL ATTORNEYS BY GROUPING

	WM	WF	BM	BF	HM	HF	AM	AF	NH/PI M	NH/PI F	AI/AN M	AI/AN F	2+M	2+F
#	31	27	2	6	1	2	5	4	0	0	0	0	0	0
%	39.7%	34.6%	2.6%	7.7%	1.3%	2.6%	6.4%	5.1%	0.0%	0.0%	0.0%	0.0%	0.0%	0.0%
CLF	57.0%	27.1%	3.7%	4.2%	1.8%	1.5%	1.5%	1.7%	0.0%	0.0%	0.0%	0.1%	0.9%	0.5%

6.7   Non-competitive promotions

At the close of FY13, 390 employees were eligible for career ladder promotions—233 were males and 157 were females. Of the 390 employees eligible, 178 received promotions and 212 did not receive promotions. Of the 178 who were eligible and received promotions, 167 received the promotion with **one to twelve months' time in grade**. The demographic breakdown of this population is:

- 58 or 37.73% White males

- 27 or 16.17% White females

- 15 or 8.98% Black males

- 31 or 18.56% Black females

- 5 or 2.99% Hispanic males

- 6 or 3.59% Hispanic females

- 10 or 5.99% Asian males

- 7 or 4.19% Asian females

- 5 or 2.99% American Indian/Alaskan Native males

- 1 or .60% American Indian/Alaskan Native females

- 1 or .60% Two or More Races male

- 1 or .60% Two or More Race female

Of the 178 eligible employees who received promotions, 4 received the promotion with thirteen to twenty-four months' time in grade, of which 3 or 75% of which were White females and 1 or 25% which were Asian females. 7 received the promotion with twenty-five or more months' time in grade, of which 2 or 28.57% were White males, 1 or 14.29% were White female, 1 or 14.29% were Black male, and 3 or 42.29% were Black females.

TABLE 23: NON-COMPETITIVE PROMOTIONS BY GENDER

	Male	Female
Eligible for Promotions	233	157
Percent (of those eligible)	59.74%	40.26%
Did Not Receive	136	76
Percent (not receiving)	**64.15%**	**35.85%**

TABLE 24: NON-COMPETITIVE PROMOTIONS BY GROUPING

	WM	WF	BM	BF	HM	HF	AM	AF	NH/PI M	NH/PI F	AI/AN M	AI/AN F	2+M	2+F
Eligible	161	73	30	52	12	12	23	18	0	0	6	1	1	1
%	41.3%	18.7%	7.7%	13.3%	3.1%	3.1%	5.9%	4.6%	0.0%	0.0%	1.5%	0.3%	0.3%	0.3%
Did Not Receive	101	42	14	18	7	6	13	10	0	0	1	0	0	0
%	47.6%	19.8%	6.6%	8.5%	3.3%	2.8%	6.1%	4.7%	0.0%	0.0%	0.5%	0.0%	0.0%	0.0%

6.8 Separations

6.8.1 Total separations

There were a total of 70 permanent employees that were separated during FY13, of which 40 or 57.14% were males and 30 or 42.86% were females. Separations include resignations, terminations, and transfers. White females at 28 or 40.00% and White males at 18 or 25.71% were the largest groups who separated from CFPB. Other rates of separation include:

- Black males – 2 or 2.86%

- Black females – 9 or 12.86%

- Hispanic males – 4 or 5.71%

- Hispanic females – 1 or 1.43%

- Asian males - 5 or 7.14%

- Asian females – 2 or 2.86%

- Male Two or More Races – 1 or 1.43%

TABLE 25: TOTAL SEPARATIONS BY GENDER

	Male	Female
Number	40	30
Percent	57.14%	42.86%

TABLE 26: TOTAL SEPARATIONS BY GROUPING

	WM	WF	BM	BF	HM	HF	AM	AF	NH/PI M	NH/PI F	AI/AN M	AI/AN F	2+M	2+F
#	28	18	2	9	4	1	5	2	0	0	0	0	1	0
%	40.0%	25.7%	2.9%	12.9%	5.7%	1.4%	7.1%	2.9%	0.0%	0.0%	0.0%	0.0%	1.4%	0.0%

6.8.2   Resignation

Of the 70 separations, 37 were resignations, the majority of which were White males (15). Other resignation rates include:

- 10 or 27.03% White females

- 3 or 8.11% Black females

- 3 or 8.11% Hispanic males

- 1 or 2.70% Hispanic females

- 2 or 5.41% Asian males

- 2 or 5.41% Asian females

- 1 or 2.70% Two or More Races female

TABLE 27: RESIGNATIONS BY GENDER

	Male	Female
Number	21	16
Percent	56.7%	43.24%

TABLE 28: RESIGNATIONS BY GROUPING

	WM	WF	BM	BF	HM	HF	AM	AF	NH/PI M	NH/PI F	AI/AN M	AI/AN F	2+M	2+F
#	15	10	0	3	3	1	2	2	0	0	0	0	1	0
%	40.5%	27.0%	0.0%	8.1%	8.1%	2.7%	5.4%	5.4%	0.0%	0.0%	0.0%	0.0%	2.7%	0.0%

6.8.3 Termination

There was 1 termination, which was a White female.

TABLE 29: TERMINATIONS BY GENDER

	Male	Female
Number	0	1
Percent	0%	100%

TABLE 30: TERMINATIONS BY GROUPING

	WM	WF	BM	BF	HM	HF	AM	AF	NH/PI M	NH/PI F	AI/AN M	AI/AN F	2+M	2+F
#	0	1	0	0	0	0	0	0	0	0	0	0	0	0
%	0.0%	100%	0.0%	0.0%	0.0%	0.0%	0.0%	0.0%	0.0%	0.0%	0.0%	0.0%	0.0%	0.0%

6.8.4 Transfer

There were 22 transfers, which consisted of 6 White males, 6 White females, 2 Black males, 4 Black females, 1 Hispanic male, and 3 Asian males.

TABLE 31: TRANSFERS BY GENDER

	Male	Female
Number	12	10
Percent	54.55%	45.45%

EEO Program Status Report for FY 2013

TABLE 32: TRANSFERS BY GROUPING

	WM	WF	BM	BF	HM	HF	AM	AF	NH/PI M	NH/PI F	AI/AN M	AI/AN F	2+M	2+F
#	6	6	2	4	1	0	3	0	0	0	0	0	0	0
%	27.2%	27.2%	9.0%	18.1%	5.6%	0.0%	13.6%	0.0%	0.0%	0.0%	0.0%	0.0%	0.0%	0.0%

6.8.5   Retirement

TABLE 33: RETIREMENTS BY GENDER

	Male	Female
Number	7	3
Percent	70%	30%

EEO Program Status Report for FY 2013

TABLE 34: RETIREMENTS BY GROUPING

	WM	WF	BM	BF	HM	HF	AM	AF	NH/PI M	NH/PI F	AI/AN M	AI/AN F	2+M	2+F
#	7	1	0	2	0	0	0	0	0	0	0	0	0	0
%	70%	10%	0.0%	20%	0.0%	0.0%	0.0%	0.0%	0.0%	0.0%	0.0%	0.0%	0.0%	0.0%

6.9   Awards

No reportable employee recognition awards were provided in FY13.

7. Certification of establishment of continuing equal employment opportunity programs

I, M. Stacey Bach, Director, Equal Employment Opportunity Office, am the Principal EEO Director/Official for the Consumer Financial Protection Bureau.

The agency has conducted an annual self-assessment of Section 717 and Section 501 programs against the essential elements as prescribed by EEO MD-715. If an essential element was not fully compliant with the standards of EEO MD-715, a further evaluation was conducted and, as appropriate, EEO Plans for Attaining the Essential Elements of a Model EEO Program, are included with this Federal Agency Annual EEO Program Status Report.

The agency has also analyzed its work force profiles and conducted barrier analyses aimed at detecting whether any management or personnel policy, procedure or practice is operating to disadvantage any group based on race, national origin, gender or disability. EEO Plans to Eliminate Identified Barriers, as appropriate, are included with this Federal Agency Annual EEO Program Status Report.

I certify that proper documentation of this assessment is in place and is being maintained for EEOC review upon request.

_____   5-28-14.

Signature of Principal EEO Director/Official   **Date**

Certifies that this Federal Agency Annual EEO Program Status Report is in compliance with EEO MD-715

_____   5/21/14

Signature of Agency Head or Agency Head Designee   **Date**

8. Federal agency annual EEO program status report

8.1 Demonstrated Commitment from Agency Leadership

FORM 715-01 PART H-1	U.S. Equal Employment Opportunity Commission FEDERAL AGENCY ANNUAL EEO PROGRAM STATUS REPORT	
Consumer Financial Protection Bureau		FY 2013
STATEMENT of MODEL PROGRAM ESSENTIAL ELEMENT DEFICIENCY:	(Part G -Q-3) Are new employees provided a copy of the EEO policy statement during orientation? During FY 2012, new employees were not routinely provided a copy of the Director's EEO policy statement at orientation.	
OBJECTIVE:	To routinely provide all new employees with Director's EEO policy statement as soon as possible.	

RESPONSIBLE OFFICIAL:	EEO Office
DATE OBJECTIVE INITIATED:	March 1, 2013
TARGET DATE FOR COMPLETION OF OBJECTIVE:	April 22, 2013

PLANNED ACTIVITIES TOWARD COMPLETION OF OBJECTIVE:	TARGET DATE (Must be specific) Completed April 2013

REPORT OF ACCOMPLISHMENTS and MODIFICATIONS TO OBJECTIVE:

As of April 2013, all persons attending new employee orientation are provided with a copy of the Director's statement and information about how to access the EEO page on the CFPB intranet, a copy of "Know Your Rights" poster, and a pamphlet describing how to file an EEO complaint in the Federal sector.

FORM 715-01 PART H-2	U.S. Equal Employment Opportunity Commission FEDERAL AGENCY ANNUAL EEO PROGRAM STATUS REPORT
Consumer Financial Protection Bureau	FY 2013
STATEMENT of MODEL PROGRAM ESSENTIAL ELEMENT	(Part G – Q-4) When an employee is promoted into the supervisory ranks, is s/he provided a copy of the EEO policy statement?

DEFICIENCY:	During FY 2012, new supervisors were not routinely provided a copy of the Director's EEO Policy statement.
OBJECTIVE:	Routinely provide supervisors and managers with the Director's statement and related EEO information.
RESPONSIBLE OFFICIAL:	EEO Office
DATE OBJECTIVE INITIATED:	March 01, 2013
TARGET DATE FOR COMPLETION OF OBJECTIVE:	April 22, 2014

PLANNED ACTIVITIES TOWARD COMPLETION OF OBJECTIVE:	TARGET DATE (Must be specific)
	Completed April 2013

REPORT OF ACCOMPLISHMENTS and MODIFICATIONS TO OBJECTIVE:

Beginning in March 2013, the EEO office instituted a process to provide new supervisors with the Director's EEO policy statement. As of April 2013, all persons attending new employee orientation are also provided with the Director's policy statement and information about how to access the EEO page on the CFPB intranet, a copy of "Know Your Rights" poster, and a pamphlet describing how to file an EEO complaint in the Federal sector.

FORM 715-01 PART H – 3	U.S. Equal Employment Opportunity Commission FEDERAL AGENCY ANNUAL EEO PROGRAM STATUS REPORT
Consumer Financial Protection Bureau	FY 2013

STATEMENT of MODEL PROGRAM ESSENTIAL ELEMENT DEFICIENCY:	(Part G - Q-19) Have the procedures for reasonable accommodation for individuals with disabilities been made readily available/accessible to all employees by disseminating such procedures during orientation of new employees and by making such procedures available on the World Wide Web or Internet? CFPB has not published information on how to request a reasonable accommodation on the Bureau's website.
OBJECTIVE:	To make CFPB's reasonable accommodation policy readily accessible.
RESPONSIBLE OFFICIAL:	EEO Director
DATE OBJECTIVE INITIATED:	April 30, 2013
TARGET DATE FOR COMPLETION OF OBJECTIVE:	September 30, 2014

PLANNED ACTIVITIES TOWARD COMPLETION OF OBJECTIVE:	TARGET DATE (Must be specific)
Publish the approved procedures on the Bureau's website.	September 2014

REPORT OF ACCOMPLISHMENTS and MODIFICATIONS TO OBJECTIVE:

CFPB's Reasonable Accommodation Procedures were submitted to EEOC for approval in January 2013, and they were approved in the Summer of 2013. The policy and procedures are readily available on the CFPB's intranet and were circulated to all employees via email. The CFPB's internet has information directing persons with disabilities to the appropriate point of contact within the Office of Human Capital; a link to the final procedures will be added.

FORM 715-01 PART H – 4	U.S. Equal Employment Opportunity Commission FEDERAL AGENCY ANNUAL EEO PROGRAM STATUS REPORT
Consumer Financial Protection Bureau	FY 2013

STATEMENT of MODEL PROGRAM ESSENTIAL ELEMENT DEFICIENCY:	(Part G - Q-20) Have the procedures for reasonable accommodation for individuals with disabilities been made readily available/accessible to all employees by disseminating such procedures during orientation of new employees and by making such procedures available on the World Wide Web or Internet?
	CFPB has not published information on how to request a reasonable accommodation on the Bureau's website.

OBJECTIVE:	To make CFPB's reasonable accommodation policy readily accessible.
RESPONSIBLE OFFICIAL:	EEO Director
DATE OBJECTIVE INITIATED:	April 30, 2013
TARGET DATE FOR COMPLETION OF OBJECTIVE:	September 30, 2014

PLANNED ACTIVITIES TOWARD COMPLETION OF OBJECTIVE:	TARGET DATE (Must be specific)
Prepare Reasonable Accommodations Procedures for submission to EEOC for approval and publish the approved procedures on the Bureau's website.	Completed January 2013

REPORT OF ACCOMPLISHMENTS and MODIFICATIONS TO OBJECTIVE:

CFPB's Reasonable Accommodation Procedures were submitted to EEOC for approval, which were approved in the Summer of 2013. The policy is readily available on the CFPB's intranet and was circulated to all employees via email. The CFPB's internet has information directing persons with disabilities to the appropriate point of contact with the Office of Human Capital; a link to the final procedures will be added.

8.2 Integration of EEO into the agency's strategic mission

FORM 715-01 PART H – 5	U.S. Equal Employment Opportunity Commission FEDERAL AGENCY ANNUAL EEO PROGRAM STATUS REPORT
Consumer Financial Protection Bureau	FY 2013

STATEMENT of MODEL PROGRAM ESSENTIAL ELEMENT DEFICIENCY:	(Part G – Q-32) Does the EEO Director have the authority and funding to ensure implementation of agency EEO action plans to improve EEO program efficiency and/or eliminate identified barriers to the realization of equality of opportunity?
	(Part G – Q-33) Are sufficient personnel resources allocated to the EEO Program to ensure that agency self-assessments and self-analyses prescribed by EEO MD-715 are conducted annually and to maintain an effective complaint processing system?
	The EEO Office needs additional staff resources. The EEO Office opened in FY13 and discussions about an organizational structure are underway.
OBJECTIVE:	To obtain sufficient resources. The approval of additional FTEs will allow the EEO Office to be fully operational and to be in compliance with EEOC's requirements for creating and maintaining a Model EEO Program.
RESPONSIBLE OFFICIAL:	EEO Director

DATE OBJECTIVE INITIATED:	April 30, 2013
TARGET DATE FOR COMPLETION OF OBJECTIVE:	September 30, 2014

PLANNED ACTIVITIES TOWARD COMPLETION OF OBJECTIVE:	TARGET DATE (Must be specific)
The EEO Director will present a case for increasing the EEO Office personnel budget to the Director and Chief Operating Officer. Increase staffing and resources for the EEO Office.	September 2014

REPORT OF ACCOMPLISHMENTS and MODIFICATIONS TO OBJECTIVE:

As the EEO Office has matured and activity has increased, new discussions about how the organizational structure of the EEO Office will meet evolving demands are underway. Discussions include the types of functions for each of the organizational components of the EEO Office, and the required staffing level to carry out mandated statutory and regulatory requirements/functions as well as creating a robust resource for proactive prevention of unlawful discrimination.

FORM 715-01 PART H – 6	U.S. Equal Employment Opportunity Commission FEDERAL AGENCY ANNUAL EEO PROGRAM STATUS REPORT
Consumer Financial Protection Bureau	FY 2013

STATEMENT of MODEL PROGRAM ESSENTIAL ELEMENT DEFICIENCY:	(Part G–Q-34) Are statutory/regulatory EEO related Special Emphasis Programs sufficiently staffed? CFPB has not yet established Special Emphasis Programs.
OBJECTIVE:	To obtain sufficient resources.
RESPONSIBLE OFFICIAL:	EEO Director
DATE OBJECTIVE INITIATED:	April 30, 2013
TARGET DATE FOR COMPLETION OF OBJECTIVE:	September 30, 2015

PLANNED ACTIVITIES TOWARD COMPLETION OF OBJECTIVE:	TARGET DATE (Must be specific)
Provide appropriate funding and resources for CFPB's EEO Office including MD-715 and Special Emphasis Programs.	September 30, 2015

Create full-time or collateral Special Emphasis Program Managers (SEPMs) to carry out the program responsibilities for the SEP programs.

REPORT OF ACCOMPLISHMENTS and MODIFICATIONS TO OBJECTIVE:

Discussions about the organizational structure of the EEO office are underway. Discussions include functional statements for each of the organizational components of the EEO Office and the required staffing level to carry out the mandated statutory and regulatory requirements/functions. This would include the appointment of Special Emphasis Program Managers or Coordinators.

FORM 715-01 PART H – 7	U.S. Equal Employment Opportunity Commission FEDERAL AGENCY ANNUAL EEO PROGRAM STATUS REPORT
Consumer Financial Protection Bureau	FY 2013
STATEMENT of MODEL PROGRAM ESSENTIAL ELEMENT DEFICIENCY:	Are statutory/regulatory EEO related Special Emphasis Programs sufficiently staffed? (Part G – Q – 35) Federal Women's Program - 5 U.S.C. 7201; 38 U.S.C. 4214; Title 5 CFR, Subpart B, 720.204 (Part G – Q – 36) Hispanic Employment Program - Title 5 CFR, Subpart B, 720.204

OBJECTIVE:	To create a Hispanic Employment Program and Federal Women's Program
RESPONSIBLE OFFICIAL:	EEO Director, OMWI Director
DATE OBJECTIVE INITIATED:	April 30, 2013
TARGET DATE FOR COMPLETION OF OBJECTIVE:	September 30, 2015

PLANNED ACTIVITIES TOWARD COMPLETION OF OBJECTIVE:	**TARGET DATE (Must be specific)**
Provide appropriate funding and resources for CFPB's EEO Office including MD-715 requirements and Special Emphasis Programs (SEP). Create full-time or collateral Special Emphasis Program Managers (SEPMs) to carry out the program responsibilities for the SEP programs.	September 30, 2015

REPORT OF ACCOMPLISHMENTS and MODIFICATIONS TO OBJECTIVE:

The Bureau has created a working group to focus on diversity recruitment, led by OMWI.

Discussions about the organizational structure of the EEO office are underway. Discussions include functional statements for each of the organizational components of the EEO office and the required staffing level to carry out the mandated statutory and regulatory requirements/functions, to include the resources for a Hispanic and Women's Program Manager/Program Coordinator.

FORM 715-01 PART H – 8	U.S. Equal Employment Opportunity Commission FEDERAL AGENCY ANNUAL EEO PROGRAM STATUS REPORT
Consumer Financial Protection Bureau	FY 2013

STATEMENT of MODEL PROGRAM ESSENTIAL ELEMENT DEFICIENCY:	(Part G – Q - 37) People With Disabilities Program Manager; Selective Placement Program for Individuals With Disabilities - Section 501 of the Rehabilitation Act; Title 5 U.S.C. Subpart B, Chapter 31, Subchapter I-3102; 5 CFR 213.3102(t) and (u); 5 CFR 315.709 CFPB does not yet have a Selective Placement Program in place.
OBJECTIVE:	To create a Selective Placement Program.
RESPONSIBLE OFFICIAL:	EEO Director, OHC Director
DATE OBJECTIVE INITIATED:	April 30, 2013
TARGET DATE FOR COMPLETION OF OBJECTIVE:	September 30, 2015
PLANNED ACTIVITIES TOWARD COMPLETION OF OBJECTIVE:	**TARGET DATE (Must be specific)**

Appoint a Human Resource Specialist to serve as the Selective Placement Specialist. The responsibilities will include: Developing ongoing plans and initiatives to address the employment of persons with targeted disabilities. Establishing hiring goals for individuals with disabilities and targeted disabilities under the Executive Order 13458.	September 30, 2014

REPORT OF ACCOMPLISHMENTS and MODIFICATIONS TO OBJECTIVE:

MODIFICATIONS TO OBJECTIVES

To establish inter-agency partnerships with other federal agencies staff responsible for the recruiting, hiring, accommodating and training of persons with disabilities.

To establish contact with the U.S. Department of Labor's Office of Disability Employment Policy (ODEP) Job Accommodation Network (JAN).

To establish contact with the State Department of Education, Division of Rehabilitation Services.

To establish contact with the Veterans Administration Medical Center.

Attend and participate in the Workforce Recruitment Program for College Students with Disabilities sponsored by the Departments of Labor and Defense.

FORM 715-01 **PART H – 9**	**U.S. Equal Employment Opportunity Commission** **FEDERAL AGENCY ANNUAL** **EEO PROGRAM STATUS REPORT**

Consumer Financial Protection Bureau	FY 2013
STATEMENT of MODEL PROGRAM ESSENTIAL ELEMENT DEFICIENCY:	(Part G – Q - 38) Are other agency special emphasis programs monitored by the EEO Office for coordination and compliance with EEO guidelines and principles, such as FEORP - 5 CFR 720; Veterans Employment Programs; and Black/African American; American Indian/Alaska Native, Asian American/Pacific Islander programs? Special Emphasis Programs at CFPB do not yet exist.
OBJECTIVE:	Establish Special Emphasis Programs
RESPONSIBLE OFFICIAL:	EEO Director, OMWI Director
DATE OBJECTIVE INITIATED:	April 30, 2013
TARGET DATE FOR COMPLETION OF OBJECTIVE:	September 30, 2015

PLANNED ACTIVITIES TOWARD COMPLETION OF OBJECTIVE:	TARGET DATE (Must be specific)
Establish an executive diversity and inclusion council.	
Prepare proposal for full-time and/or establish collateral duty Special Emphasis Program Managers (SEPM).	September 30, 2014
Develop a SEPM informational kit with general information about SEP programs and responsibilities.	
Show visible support of SEP programs by attending and providing remarks at SEP activities and observances.	
Develop Standard Operating Procedures (SOP) on managing special emphasis programs within CFPB.	
Establish collaboration between EEO, OMWI, and EA to identify roles and responsibilities in coordinating observances and commemorative events.	
Establish partnership with employees' professional groups and support participation in employees' affinity groups.	

FORM 715-01 PART H – 10	U.S. Equal Employment Opportunity Commission FEDERAL AGENCY ANNUAL EEO PROGRAM STATUS REPORT
Consumer Financial Protection Bureau	FY 2013

STATEMENT of MODEL PROGRAM ESSENTIAL ELEMENT DEFICIENCY:	(Part G – Q – 40) Is there sufficient budget allocated to all employees to utilize, when desired, all EEO programs, including the complaint processing program and ADR, and to make a request for reasonable accommodation? (Including subordinate level reporting components?) (Part G – Q – 41) Has funding been secured for publication and distribution of EEO materials (e.g. harassment policies, EEO posters, reasonable accommodations procedures, etc.)?
OBJECTIVE:	To obtain ample staff to provide EEO training.
RESPONSIBLE OFFICIAL:	EEO Director
DATE OBJECTIVE INITIATED:	April 30, 2013
TARGET DATE FOR COMPLETION OF OBJECTIVE:	September 30, 2014

PLANNED ACTIVITIES TOWARD COMPLETION OF OBJECTIVE:	**TARGET DATE**

	(Must be specific)

REPORT OF ACCOMPLISHMENTS and MODIFICATIONS TO OBJECTIVE:

The EEO Office opened in FY13 and discussions about adjusting the organizational structure and budget are underway. The EEO Office obtained full- time and contract support during FY13 and FY14. The office will continue to use external training options and informal training opportunities (such as fliers sent to all employees and available on the CFPB intranet) to provide EEO information.

Online No FEAR and sexual harassment training is provided to all new employees and required for existing employees.

FORM 715-01 PART H – 11	U.S. Equal Employment Opportunity Commission FEDERAL AGENCY ANNUAL EEO PROGRAM STATUS REPORT
Consumer Financial Protection Bureau	FY 2013

STATEMENT of MODEL PROGRAM ESSENTIAL ELEMENT DEFICIENCY:	(Part G – Q - 46) Is there funding to ensure that all employees have access to this training and information? (Part G – Q - 47) Is there sufficient funding to provide all managers and supervisors with training and periodic up-dates on their EEO responsibilities?
OBJECTIVE:	To obtain ample staff to provide EEO training.
RESPONSIBLE OFFICIAL:	EEO Director, OHC Director

DATE OBJECTIVE INITIATED:	April 30, 2013
TARGET DATE FOR COMPLETION OF OBJECTIVE:	September 30, 2015

PLANNED ACTIVITIES TOWARD COMPLETION OF OBJECTIVE:	TARGET DATE (Must be specific)
Obtain reports from OHC regarding employees and managers taking No Fear and Sexual Harassment training. Develop and implement mandatory EEO compliance training for managers and supervisors. Ensure that all training programs are Section 508 compliant. Offer Reasonable Accommodation training. Partner with OHC to develop and incorporate EEO training in all leadership training modules and emerging leaders training programs.	September 30, 2015

REPORT OF ACCOMPLISHMENTS and MODIFICATIONS TO OBJECTIVE:

The EEO Office obtained full- time and contract support during FY13 and FY14. Pending additional staff in the EEO Office, the office will continue to use external training options (e.g., NELI, EEOC Training Institute, FELTG) and informal training opportunities (such as fliers sent to all employees and available on the CFPB intranet) to provide EEO information.

Online No FEAR Act training is provided to all new employees and all CFPB's employees are required to take the No FEAR Act training every two years. Sexual harassment prevention training is required within 90 days of employment with CFPB. Also, employees are required to take sexual harassment prevention training every two years.

In-house training modules for hiring in compliance with the law and an EEO overview have been created. A one-hour segment on EEO laws has also been included in OHC's supervisory training module.

FORM 715-01 PART H – 12	U.S. Equal Employment Opportunity Commission FEDERAL AGENCY ANNUAL EEO PROGRAM STATUS REPORT
Consumer Financial Protection Bureau	FY 2013

STATEMENT of MODEL PROGRAM ESSENTIAL ELEMENT DEFICIENCY:	(Part G – Q – 50) to provide disability accommodations in accordance with the agency's written procedures? CFPB does not yet track compliance with the procedures set forth in a Reasonable Accommodation policy.
OBJECTIVE:	To track compliance with procedures.
RESPONSIBLE OFFICIAL:	EEO Director
DATE OBJECTIVE INITIATED:	April 30, 2013
TARGET DATE FOR COMPLETION OF OBJECTIVE:	September 30, 2016

PLANNED ACTIVITIES TOWARD COMPLETION OF OBJECTIVE:	TARGET DATE (Must be specific)
Establish Reasonable Accommodation team consisting of EEO, OHC, and the Federal Occupational Health (FOH) Service.	September 30, 2015

EEO, OMWI and OHC participate on committees to address building and facility accommodation/accessibility issues.	September 30, 2015
Incorporate entelliTrak data management system into daily operations.	September 30, 2015

REPORT OF ACCOMPLISHMENTS and MODIFICATIONS TO OBJECTIVE:

CFPB received and processed 25 requests for reasonable accommodations during FY13.

CFPB held training sessions entitled "Human Resource Guide to American With Disabilities Act (ADA) Workplace" facilitated by the National Employment Law Institute, Director of ADA and EEO, David K. Fram, Esq.,

The CFPB's Reasonable Accommodation Policy was approved by the EEOC pursuant to Executive Order 13164 in the Summer of 2013 and distributed to employees in July 2013. CFPB has begun to track decisions to ensure compliance with procedures and timeframes.

CFPB is reviewing possible tracking systems that can be used to track compliance with reasonable accommodation procedures and to monitor the status of reasonable accommodation requests.

8.3 Management and Program Accountability

FORM 715-01	U.S. Equal Employment Opportunity Commission
	FEDERAL AGENCY ANNUAL
PART H – 13	EEO PROGRAM STATUS REPORT

Consumer Financial Protection Bureau		FY 2013
STATEMENT of MODEL PROGRAM ESSENTIAL ELEMENT DEFICIENCY:	(Part G – Q – 53) Are regular (monthly/quarterly/semi-annually) EEO updates provided to management/supervisory officials by EEO program officials? (Part G – Q – 54) Do EEO program officials coordinate the development and implementation of EEO Plans with all appropriate agency managers to include Agency Counsel, Hum Resources Officials, Finance, and the Chief Information Officer? To date, the EEO Office has not met with senior managers to identify barriers that may be impeding the realization of equal employment opportunity. The EEO Office intends to begin such meetings in FY13 and FY14.	
OBJECTIVE:	Meet with senior managers to identify barriers that may be impeding the realization of equal employment opportunity.	
RESPONSIBLE OFFICIAL:	EEO Director, OHC Director	
DATE OBJECTIVE INITIATED:	April 30, 2013	
PLANNED ACTIVITIES TOWARD COMPLETION OF OBJECTIVE:		TARGET DATE (Must be specific)
Director of EEO will meet with CHCO to re-affirm an internal review process for EEO to review drafts of proposed policies, procedures		September 30, 2014

and practices prior to finalizing the drafts.	
EEO will develop a yearly implementation plan to review selected policies, procedures, and practices.	September 30, 2014

REPORT OF ACCOMPLISHMENTS and MODIFICATIONS TO OBJECTIVE:

MODIFICATIONS TO OBJECTIVE

To assess whether there are any hidden impediments to equality of opportunity, the EEO Office will examine on regular intervals management/personnel policies, procedures and practices.

Develop ad hoc barrier analysis and evaluative reports for organizational components.

Identify barriers (hiring, promotions, retention, evaluations, awards) affecting the CFPB workforce and implement corrective actions to resolve undesired conditions, if any.

Respond to requests for workforce analyses information related to EEO complaints.

Participate and collaborate on CFPB committees as a subject matter expert, i.e., awards, selection panels, performance reviews, etc., to address issues related to adequate representation of all EEO groups and possible adverse impacts on protected groups.

Increase EEO participation role on internal and external committees.

Identify workforce barriers and propose corrective actions.

FORM 715-01	U.S. Equal Employment Opportunity Commission
PART H – 14	FEDERAL AGENCY ANNUAL EEO PROGRAM STATUS REPORT

Consumer Financial Protection Bureau	FY 2013
STATEMENT of MODEL PROGRAM ESSENTIAL ELEMENT DEFICIENCY:	(Part G – Q - 63) Do senior managers meet with and assist the EEO Director and/or other EEO Program Officials in the identification of barriers that may be impeding the realization of equal employment opportunity? (Part G – Q - 64) When barriers are identified, do senior managers develop and implement, with the assistance of the agency EEO office, agency EEO Action Plans to eliminate said barriers? This report contains the CFPB's first barrier analysis, so senior managers have not yet had an opportunity to implement EEO Action Plans.
OBJECTIVE:	Establish collaboration with senior managers to develop corrective action plans as needed.
RESPONSIBLE OFFICIAL:	EEO Director, Senior Managers
DATE OBJECTIVE INITIATED:	April 30, 2013
TARGET DATE FOR COMPLETION OF OBJECTIVE:	September 30, 2014

PLANNED ACTIVITIES TOWARD COMPLETION OF OBJECTIVE:	TARGET DATE (Must be specific)

The EEO will deliver the annual "State of The Agency" briefing to CFPB's Director and leadership upon completion and submission of the FY13 MD-715 report.	May/June 2014

REPORT OF ACCOMPLISHMENTS and MODIFICATIONS TO OBJECTIVE:

The EEO Director attends weekly scheduled Operations (OPS) meeting where updates are provided to managers on current issues involving EEO matters.

The EEO Director provides EEO updates at the Operations Advisory Committee (OAC).

EEO worked in collaboration with OMWI and OHC in preparing the annual Federal Equal Opportunity Recruitment Plan (FEORP) and the Disabled Veterans Affirmative Action Plan (DVAAP).

EEO provides input into the annual Office of Minority and Women Inclusion (OMWI) report to Congress.

8.4   Proactive Prevention

FORM 715-01 PART H – 15	U.S. Equal Employment Opportunity Commission FEDERAL AGENCY ANNUAL EEO PROGRAM STATUS REPORT
Consumer Financial Protection Bureau	FY 2013
STATEMENT of MODEL PROGRAM ESSENTIAL ELEMENT DEFICIENCY:	(Part G – Q - 66) Are trend analyses of workforce profiles conducted by race, national origin, sex and disability? (Part G – Q - 67) Are trend analyses of the workforce's major occupations conducted by race, national origin, sex and disability? (Part G – Q - 68) Are trends analyses of the workforce's grade level distribution conducted by race, national origin, sex and disability?

	(Part G – Q – 69) Are trend analyses of the workforce's compensation and reward system conducted by race, national origin, sex and disability? (Part G – Q – 70) Are trend analyses of the effects of management/personnel policies, procedures and practices conducted by race, national origin, sex and disability?
OBJECTIVE:	Develop ad hoc barrier analysis and evaluative reports.
RESPONSIBLE OFFICIAL:	EEO Director
DATE OBJECTIVE INITIATED:	April 30, 2013
TARGET DATE FOR COMPLETION OF OBJECTIVE:	September 30, 2014

PLANNED ACTIVITIES TOWARD COMPLETION OF OBJECTIVE:	TARGET DATE (Must be specific)
Meet quarterly with Office Director to discuss trends, issues and training needs. Develop quarterly ad hoc reports reflecting the workplace issues for each Office Director. Perform bi-annual analysis of conflict trends, impact analysis.	September 30, 2015

REPORT OF ACCOMPLISHMENTS and MODIFICATIONS TO OBJECTIVE:

FORM 715-01 PART H – 16	U.S. Equal Employment Opportunity Commission FEDERAL AGENCY ANNUAL EEO PROGRAM STATUS REPORT
Consumer Financial Protection Bureau	FY 2013

STATEMENT of MODEL PROGRAM ESSENTIAL ELEMENT DEFICIENCY:	(Part G – Q - 71) Are all employees encouraged to use ADR? (Part G – Q - 91) In accordance with 29 C.F.R. §1614.102(b), has the agency established an ADR Program during the pre-complaint and formal complaint stages of the EEO process?
OBJECTIVE:	To establish an ADR Program and Policy.
RESPONSIBLE OFFICIAL:	EEO Director
DATE OBJECTIVE INITIATED:	April 30, 2013
TARGET DATE FOR COMPLETION OF OBJECTIVE:	September 30, 2014

PLANNED ACTIVITIES TOWARD COMPLETION OF OBJECTIVE:	TARGET DATE (Must be specific)
Promote the use of Alternative Dispute Resolution (ADR) for early dispute resolution.	September 30, 2015

Continue to build collaborative relationship with Employee and Labor Relations and Legal Division for resolution outcomes during mediations.	September 30, 2015
Develop a variety of informative brochures, media campaigns, emails that promote ADR.	September 30, 2015

REPORT OF ACCOMPLISHMENTS and MODIFICATIONS TO OBJECTIVE:

The EEO Office has a robust ADR program in place. The EEO Office is offering ADR during the informal and formal stage of the EEO complaint process through a cadre of contract mediators. Information on ADR is available on intranet and has been circulated to employers.

8.5 Efficiency

FORM 715-01 PART H – 17	U.S. Equal Employment Opportunity Commission FEDERAL AGENCY ANNUAL EEO PROGRAM STATUS REPORT
Consumer Financial Protection Bureau	FY 2013

STATEMENT of MODEL PROGRAM ESSENTIAL ELEMENT DEFICIENCY:	(Part G – Q - 92) Does the agency require all managers and supervisors to receive ADR training in accordance with EEOC (29 C.F.R. Part 1614) regulations, with emphasis on the federal government's interest in encouraging mutual resolution of disputes and the benefits associated with utilizing ADR? The CFPB has not trained supervisors and managers about ADR. The EEO Office was established in February 2013 and has not yet offered training about ADR to managers. It expects to do so by the end of FY 2014.
OBJECTIVE:	To train supervisors and managers about ADR.
RESPONSIBLE OFFICIAL:	EEO Director
DATE OBJECTIVE INITIATED:	April 30, 2014
TARGET DATE FOR COMPLETION OF OBJECTIVE:	September 30, 2014

PLANNED ACTIVITIES TOWARD COMPLETION OF OBJECTIVE:	TARGET DATE (Must be specific)
Develop customized training modules upon request regarding conflict resolution, effective communication, teambuilding, interpersonal skills training and other workplace situation that could potentially give rise to conflict.	September 30, 2014

REPORT OF ACCOMPLISHMENTS and MODIFICATIONS TO OBJECTIVE:

Information on ADR is available on intranet and was circulated to employees.

FORM 715-01 PART H – 18	U.S. Equal Employment Opportunity Commission FEDERAL AGENCY ANNUAL EEO PROGRAM STATUS REPORT
Consumer Financial Protection Bureau	FY 2013

STATEMENT of MODEL PROGRAM ESSENTIAL ELEMENT DEFICIENCY:	(Part G – Q - 94) Does the responsible management official directly involved in the dispute have settlement authority? The responsible management official involved in the EEO dispute does not have settlement authority because a CFPB delegation of authority provides the Legal Division with settlement authority for EEO cases at the administrative level.
OBJECTIVE:	To obtain delegation of authority for senior officials to have settlement authority during EEO complaint negotiations.
RESPONSIBLE OFFICIAL:	EEO Director
DATE OBJECTIVE INITIATED:	April 30, 2013
TARGET DATE FOR COMPLETION OF OBJECTIVE:	September 30, 2014

PLANNED ACTIVITIES TOWARD COMPLETION OF OBJECTIVE:	TARGET DATE

	(Must be specific)
Meet with the Legal Division to discuss delegation of authority for senior management officials for settlement of EEO complaints.	September 30, 2014

REPORT OF ACCOMPLISHMENTS and MODIFICATIONS TO OBJECTIVE:

FORM 715-01 PART H – 19	U.S. Equal Employment Opportunity Commission FEDERAL AGENCY ANNUAL EEO PROGRAM STATUS REPORT
Consumer Financial Protection Bureau	FY 2013
STATEMENT of MODEL PROGRAM ESSENTIAL ELEMENT DEFICIENCY:	(Part G – Q – 102) Are legal sufficiency reviews of EEO matters handled by a functional unit that is separate and apart from the unit which handles agency representation in EEO complaints?
OBJECTIVE:	To ensure that a functional unit that is separate and apart from the unit that handles agency representation conducts legal sufficiency reviews.
RESPONSIBLE OFFICIAL:	EEO Director, Director Legal Division, Office of General Law and Ethics
DATE OBJECTIVE	

INITIATED:	April 30, 2013
TARGET DATE FOR COMPLETION OF OBJECTIVE:	September 30, 2014

PLANNED ACTIVITIES TOWARD COMPLETION OF OBJECTIVE:	TARGET DATE (Must be specific)
	September 30, 2014

REPORT OF ACCOMPLISHMENTS and MODIFICATIONS TO OBJECTIVE:

The Legal Division does not conduct sufficiency reviews of EEO office matters including accept/dismiss letters, ROIs, or Final Agency Decisions.

8.6 Responsiveness and Legal Compliance

FORM 715-01 PART H – 20	U.S. Equal Employment Opportunity Commission FEDERAL AGENCY ANNUAL EEO PROGRAM STATUS REPORT	
Consumer Financial Protection Bureau		FY 2013
STATEMENT of MODEL PROGRAM ESSENTIAL ELEMENT	(Part G – Q – 109) Is compliance with EEOC orders encompassed in the performance standards of any agency employees?	

DEFICIENCY:	
OBJECTIVE:	Ensure performance standards contain metrics to measure compliance with EEOC orders.
RESPONSIBLE OFFICIAL:	EEO Director, OHC
DATE OBJECTIVE INITIATED:	April 30, 2013
TARGET DATE FOR COMPLETION OF OBJECTIVE:	September 30, 2015

PLANNED ACTIVITIES TOWARD COMPLETION OF OBJECTIVE:	TARGET DATE (Must be specific)
Ensure the EEO Office participates in discussions for the upcoming modifications to the performance management system. Ensure that any EEO proposed language and/or compliance standards are reviewed and included in the new performance management standards. Ensure the EEO Office serves as a team member on the education team to roll out the new performance management system.	September 30, 2015

REPORT OF ACCOMPLISHMENTS and MODIFICATIONS TO OBJECTIVE:

The EEO office will be part of a working group with OHC, OMWI, and NTEU to assess the performance management system and review ratings distributions.

FORM 715-01 PART H – 21	U.S. Equal Employment Opportunity Commission FEDERAL AGENCY ANNUAL EEO PROGRAM STATUS REPORT
Consumer Financial Protection Bureau	FY 2013

STATEMENT of MODEL PROGRAM ESSENTIAL ELEMENT DEFICIENCY:	(Part G – Q – 110) Is the unit charged with the responsibility for compliance with EEOC orders located in the EEO office? The unit charged with responsibility for complying with EEOC orders has not yet been defined
OBJECTIVE:	To specify that the EEO Office is charged with the responsibility for ensuring compliance with EEO orders.
RESPONSIBLE OFFICIAL:	EEO Director
DATE OBJECTIVE INITIATED:	April 30, 2013
TARGET DATE FOR COMPLETION OF OBJECTIVE:	September 30, 2014

PLANNED ACTIVITIES TOWARD COMPLETION OF OBJECTIVE:	TARGET DATE (Must be specific)

Establish collaboration with the Legal Division to ensure compliance with EEOC orders.	September 30, 2014
REPORT OF ACCOMPLISHMENTS and MODIFICATIONS TO OBJECTIVE:	

9. Barrier Analysis

EEOC FORM 715-01 PART I-1	U.S. Equal Employment Opportunity Commission FEDERAL AGENCY ANNUAL EEO PROGRAM STATUS REPORT
Consumer Financial Protection Bureau	**New Hires** <u>2014</u> <u>FY</u>
STATEMENT OF CONDITION THAT WAS A TRIGGER FOR A POTENTIAL BARRIER: Provide a brief narrative describing the condition at issue. How was the condition recognized as a potential barrier?	Data comparisons between the 2010 Civilian Labor Force (CLF), application, qualification, and selection rates in some major occupations revealed instances of lower-than-anticipated selection rates for some groups in CFPB's critical occupations.
BARRIER ANALYSIS: Provide a description of the steps taken and data analyzed to determine cause of the condition.	CFPB reviewed the statistical data associated with new hires as well as the graphical representation of the data for the Bureau's critical occupations. **A. Application** In comparing the CLF to the applicant rate, it appears that CFPB

experienced a degree of success in its recruitment efforts. For example, for the Economist (0110) occupation series, CFPB received a total of 1285 applications where 1195 applicants voluntarily identified their demographic profile. Of those applications received, 932 (641 males or 68.80% and 291 females or 31.20%) were found qualified. All groups with the exception of White males and White females, Native Hawaiian/Pacific Islanders males and females, American Indian/Alaskan Native females were qualified at rates higher than their representation in the CLF for positions in the (0110) series.

B. Selection

There is some positive news in terms of selections: 3 Hispanic males or 8.8% and 1 Hispanic female or 2.9% were hired compared to CLFs or 3.3% and 1.8% respectively.

STATEMENT OF IDENTIFIED BARRIER: Provide a succinct statement of the agency policy, procedure or practice that has been determined to be the barrier of the undesired condition.	At this time, it is not possible to identify a specific policy, practice or procedure that may be causing any of the identified lower-than-expected participation rates. But, the data suggests that CFPB should continue to examine its recruitment policies and practices for the 0110, 0301, 0570 and 0905 series to determine why some individuals, although their qualifications rates are higher than their availability in the CLF, are being selected at rates lower than the CLF availability.
OBJECTIVE: State the alternative or revised agency policy, procedure or practice to be implemented to correct the undesired condition.	CFPB will continue its analysis of the hiring process, including recruitment, qualification and selection, associated with the above-identified lower-than-expected participation rates for several occupational series.
RESPONSIBLE OFFICIAL:	EEO, OWMI, OHC, Managers and Supervisors throughout the Bureau

DATE OBJECTIVE INITIATED:	May 2014
TARGET DATE FOR COMPLETION OF OBJECTIVE:	September 30, 2014

PLANNED ACTIVITIES TOWARD COMPLETION OF OBJECTIVE:	TARGET DATE (Must be specific)
OHC will continue to deliver its hiring tool kit to support the managers and in-person presentations by representatives of the recruitment staff on hiring flexibilities, and selection processes.	September 30, 2014
EEO and OWMI will develop a plan for assessing whether there are attitudinal barriers to selection opportunities by meetings with Special Emphasis Program groups, OHC recruiting teams, and other managers and employees.	
EEO, OHC, and OWMI will conduct a deeper assessment of the Annual Employee Survey (AES) to support identification of procedural barriers that may exist in the development of vacancy announcements and the conduct of outreach efforts.	

REPORT OF ACCOMPLISHMENTS and MODIFICATIONS TO OBJECTIVE

OMWI and the EEO Office each developed and delivered hiring training in October 2013 to SEFL managers – the largest CFPB division.

OHC is now tracking additional application-related data (declination rates and reasons, persons selected to be interviewed) for further assessment.

EEOC FORM 715-01 PART I-2	U.S. Equal Employment Opportunity Commission FEDERAL AGENCY ANNUAL EEO PROGRAM STATUS REPORT
Consumer Financial Protection Bureau	**Participation Rates** FY 2014

STATEMENT OF CONDITION THAT WAS A TRIGGER FOR A POTENTIAL BARRIER: Provide a brief narrative describing the condition at issue. How was the condition recognized as a potential barrier?	Data comparisons between the Civilian Labor Force (CLF) and participation rates revealed instances where participation rates for White females at 28.29%, Hispanic males at 2.76%, Hispanic females at 2.68%, American Indian/Alaskan Natives males at 0.45%, American Indian/Alaskan Natives at 0.22% and Two or More Races males at 0.22% were below their CLF availability.
BARRIER ANALYSIS: Provide a description of the steps taken and data analyzed to determine cause of the condition.	CFPB reviewed the statistical data associated with (Table A1) as well as the graphical representation of the data for the Bureau's major occupations.
STATEMENT OF IDENTIFIED BARRIER: Provide a succinct statement of the agency policy, procedure or practice that has been determined to be the barrier of the undesired condition.	Although there was no barrier identified for this trigger, CFPB will continue to monitor participation rates and recommend outreach to targeted groups as appropriate.

OBJECTIVE: State the alternative or revised agency policy, procedure or practice to be implemented to correct the undesired condition.	Monitor participation rates to ensure CFPB hiring of groups where participation rates are below CLF.
RESPONSIBLE OFFICIAL:	EEO, OWMI, OHC
DATE OBJECTIVE INITIATED:	May 2014
TARGET DATE FOR COMPLETION OF OBJECTIVE:	September 30, 2014

PLANNED ACTIVITIES TOWARD COMPLETION OF OBJECTIVE:	TARGET DATE (Must be specific)
Analyze applicant flow data and monitor selection process to ensure applicants rates, qualification rates, and selection rates are consistent with CLF availability. Complete initial trends analysis of workforce profiles to identify additional triggers. Ensure that the Bureau considers whether any group of employees or applicant might be negatively impacted prior to making human capital decisions.	September 30, 2014

REPORT OF ACCOMPLISHMENTS and MODIFICATIONS TO OBJECTIVE

EEOC FORM 715-01 PART I-3	U.S. Equal Employment Opportunity Commission FEDERAL AGENCY ANNUAL EEO PROGRAM STATUS REPORT
Consumer Financial Protection Bureau	**EEO Office Resources** 2014 <u>FY</u>
STATEMENT OF CONDITION THAT WAS A TRIGGER FOR A POTENTIAL BARRIER: Provide a brief narrative describing the condition at issue. How was the condition recognized as a potential barrier?	Adequate personnel resources may not yet be allocated to the EEO program to ensure that CFPB can perform all the requirements of an EEO Model Program as prescribed by MD-715.
BARRIER ANALYSIS: Provide a description of the steps taken and	The EEO Office, opened in February 2013, may not yet have resources that will be available in steady-state and the duties and responsibilities of the EEO office and its staff have not been clearly defined between it, OMWI, and OHC.

data analyzed to determine cause of the condition.	
STATEMENT OF IDENTIFIED BARRIER: Provide a succinct statement of the agency policy, procedure or practice that has been determined to be the barrier of the undesired condition.	The office may not yet be fully resourced and clear roles and responsibilities do not yet exist.
OBJECTIVE: State the alternative or revised agency policy, procedure or practice to be implemented to correct the undesired condition.	To ensure that sufficient personnel resources are allocated to the EEO Program to enable CFPB's EEO program to become a model EEO program. To ensure that mandated Special Emphasis Programs are sufficiently staffed. To obtain sufficient resources to continue ongoing mandated barrier analysis.
RESPONSIBLE OFFICIAL:	EEO, OHC, COO
DATE OBJECTIVE INITIATED:	May 2014
TARGET DATE FOR COMPLETION OF OBJECTIVE:	September 30, 2014

PLANNED ACTIVITIES TOWARD COMPLETION OF OBJECTIVE:	
Prepare a justification for budget and staffing needs/gap assessment based on CFPB's size and scope of responsibility and present to the Director and COO. Clearly define the responsibilities and duties of the EEO office and EEO staff, including the EEO/OWMI cross-functional areas of affirmative employment, special emphasis programs, training, data analysis, and targeted outreach. Identify and utilize resources that do not require additional budget or required additional FTEs such as rotational assignments, detail assignments and leveraging partnerships with other entities. Develop a schedule and conduct regular and effective means for the EEO Director to inform CFPB's Director and leadership of the EEO program's statutory and regulatory requirements and the need for resources to meet those requirements. Staff and provide the needed resources to have effective statutory special emphasis programs and program managers. Ensure that the EEO Director is included in strategic planning, human capital planning processes, succession planning, training and development planning, etc. to ensure EEO concerns are integrated into the agency strategic mission	**TARGET DATE** **(Must be specific)** September 30, 2014

REPORT OF ACCOMPLISHMENTS and MODIFICATIONS TO OBJECTIVE

EEOC FORM 715-01 PART I-4	U.S. *Equal Employment Opportunity Commission* **FEDERAL AGENCY ANNUAL** **EEO PROGRAM STATUS REPORT**
Consumer Financial Protection Bureau	**EEO Compliance Training** <u>FY</u> <u>2014</u>
STATEMENT OF CONDITION THAT WAS A TRIGGER FOR A POTENTIAL BARRIER: Provide a brief narrative describing the condition at issue. How was the condition recognized as a potential barrier?	CFPB has not provided and/or required live EEO compliance training of all managers, supervisors and employees in the areas of: • EEO overview training for managers • Reasonable accommodations procedures and responsibilities • Workplace harassment and retaliation • Alternative Dispute Resolution
BARRIER ANALYSIS: Provide a description of the steps taken and data analyzed to determine cause of the condition.	Ensure that sufficient resources are provided to the EEO Program so that EEO training is delivered to all employees, especially managers and supervisors. To ensure all CFPB's managers, supervisors and employees receive appropriate EEO compliance training.
STATEMENT OF IDENTIFIED BARRIER:	The EEO Office was established in February 2013. Current staff resources cannot support dedicating an FTE to EEO training.

Provide a succinct statement of the agency policy, procedure or practice that has been determined to be the barrier of the undesired condition.	
OBJECTIVE: State the alternative or revised agency policy, procedure or practice to be implemented to correct the undesired condition.	Ensure that sufficient resources (staff or funding) so that EEO training is delivered to all employees, especially managers and Supervisors. To ensure all CFPB's managers, supervisors and employees receive appropriate EEO compliance training.
RESPONSIBLE OFFICIAL:	EEO
DATE OBJECTIVE INITIATED:	May 2014
TARGET DATE FOR COMPLETION OF OBJECTIVE:	September 30, 2014

PLANNED ACTIVITIES TOWARD COMPLETION OF OBJECTIVE:	TARGET DATE (Must be specific)
.	

	September 30, 2014
EEO Director schedule regular and ongoing EEO briefings and updates to CFPB's Director, Executives, Managers and Supervisors.	
REPORT OF ACCOMPLISHMENTS and MODIFICATIONS TO OBJECTIVE	

EEOC FORM 715-01 PART I-5	U.S. Equal Employment Opportunity Commission FEDERAL AGENCY ANNUAL EEO PROGRAM STATUS REPORT
Consumer Financial Protection Bureau	**Performance Management** <u>FY</u> <u>2014</u>

STATEMENT OF CONDITION THAT WAS A TRIGGER FOR A POTENTIAL BARRIER: Provide a brief narrative describing the condition at issue. How was the condition recognized as a potential barrier?	A review of performance ratings for FY13 revealed that non-minorities and persons under 40 received higher ratings than minorities especially, Blacks, Hispanics and persons 40 years and over. Performance ratings are tied to CFPB's pay-for-performance system.
BARRIER ANALYSIS: Provide a description of the steps taken and data analyzed to determine cause of the condition.	CFPB conducted an analysis of performance rating distributions.
STATEMENT OF IDENTIFIED BARRIER: Provide a succinct statement of the agency policy,	Although there is not yet enough information to determine whether an actual barrier exists for this trigger, the EEO Office, OMWI, and OHC, along with a third party contractor, will review additional statistics, files, and/or the Performance Management System to ascertain additional information for assessing the trigger.

procedure or practice that has been determined to be the barrier of the undesired condition.	
OBJECTIVE: State the alternative or revised agency policy, procedure or practice to be implemented to correct the undesired condition.	Analyze the results of the Performance Management System to determine if there is adverse impact on minorities and employees over 40.
RESPONSIBLE OFFICIAL:	EEO, OWMI, OHC, LR
DATE OBJECTIVE INITIATED:	May 2014
TARGET DATE FOR COMPLETION OF OBJECTIVE:	September 30, 2014

PLANNED ACTIVITIES TOWARD COMPLETION OF OBJECTIVE:	TARGET DATE (Must be specific)
Obtain statistics and related files to analyze performance ratings for FY13. Analyze the performance rating data and related files to determine whether the difference in the rating can be attributable to legitimate causes.	September 30, 2014

REPORT OF ACCOMPLISHMENTS and MODIFICATIONS TO OBJECTIVE

Engaging third party contractor to further assess data.

Leadership team, led by COO, assembled.

Current system will be renegotiated with NTEU.

EEOC FORM 715-01 PART I-6	U.S. Equal Employment Opportunity Commission FEDERAL AGENCY ANNUAL EEO PROGRAM STATUS REPORT
Consumer Financial Protection Bureau	**Career Ladder Promotions** <u>FY</u> <u>2014</u>
STATEMENT OF CONDITION THAT WAS A TRIGGER FOR A POTENTIAL BARRIER:	At the close of FY 2013, 390 employees were eligible for career ladder promotions - 233 males and 157 females. Of the 390 employees eligible, 178 received promotions and 212 did not receive promotions. An analysis of the career ladder promotions revealed that CFPB has 4 employees with 13 to 24 months-time in grade without receiving career ladder promotions. All 4 employees are females -- 3 or 75.00% White females and 1 or 25.00% Black

Provide a brief narrative describing the condition at issue. How was the condition recognized as a potential barrier?	female. In addition, there are 7 employees with 25 plus months- time in grade -- 3 males (42.96%) and 4 females (57.14%.) There are 2 White males, 1 White female, 1 Black male and 3 Black females.
BARRIER ANALYSIS: Provide a description of the steps taken and data analyzed to determine cause of the condition.	CFPB conducted an analysis of non-competitive promotions to determine if there were any disparities in promotions.
STATEMENT OF IDENTIFIED BARRIER: Provide a succinct statement of the agency policy, procedure or practice that has been determined to be the barrier of the undesired condition.	Although there was no barrier identified, CFPB notes that there were only 10 employees that had 25 months plus in career ladder positions that had not received promotions.
OBJECTIVE: State the alternative or revised agency policy, procedure or practice to be implemented to correct the undesired condition.	CFPB will conduct a review of the Bureau's policy on career ladder promotions to determine if the policy is administered equitably across all groups..

RESPONSIBLE OFFICIAL:	EEO, OWMI, OHC
DATE OBJECTIVE INITIATED:	May 2014
TARGET DATE FOR COMPLETION OF OBJECTIVE:	September 30, 2015

PLANNED ACTIVITIES TOWARD COMPLETION OF OBJECTIVE:	TARGET DATE (Must be specific)
Conduct a comprehensive review of CFPB's career ladder promotions policies and procedures to determine whether any barriers exist in CFPB's hiring and/or promotion practices.	September 30, 2015
REPORT OF ACCOMPLISHMENTS and MODIFICATIONS TO OBJECTIVE	

EEOC FORM 715-01 PART I-7	U.S. Equal Employment Opportunity Commission FEDERAL AGENCY ANNUAL EEO PROGRAM STATUS REPORT
Consumer Financial Protection Bureau	**Person With Disabilities** <u>FY</u> <u>2014</u>

STATEMENT OF CONDITION THAT WAS A TRIGGER FOR A POTENTIAL BARRIER: Provide a brief narrative describing the condition at issue. How was the condition recognized as a potential barrier?	The participation rates of Individuals with Disabilities in CFPB's workforce increased from 6 persons or 0.61% to 9 persons or 0.67%, which is an increase of 3 and a net change of 50%.
BARRIER ANALYSIS: Provide a description of the steps taken and data analyzed to determine cause of the condition.	CFPB conducted an analysis of Workforce Table B-1.
STATEMENT OF IDENTIFIED BARRIER: Provide a succinct statement of the agency policy,	There were no barriers identified for this trigger, CFPB made 6 selections of persons with disabilities and the overall participation rate is increasing.

procedure or practice that has been determined to be the barrier of the undesired condition.	
OBJECTIVE: State the alternative or revised agency policy, procedure or practice to be implemented to correct the undesired condition.	Increase the number of persons with disabilities at CFPB and increase the number of persons with targeted disabilities to 2.0% and effectively integrate all persons with disabilities into the CFPB workforce.
RESPONSIBLE OFFICIAL:	EEO, OWMI, OHC
DATE OBJECTIVE INITIATED:	September 30, 2014
TARGET DATE FOR COMPLETION OF OBJECTIVE:	September 30, 2014

PLANNED ACTIVITIES TOWARD COMPLETION OF OBJECTIVE: Develop an awareness campaign for hiring persons with disabilities and persons with targeted disabilities. Promote and utilize the Schedule A hiring authorities.	TARGET DATE (Must be specific) September 30, 2014

Provide training to supervisors and managers on their responsibilities to encourage hiring of persons with disabilities and persons with targeted disabilities.

Provide training to managers and supervisors on their responsibilities to provide reasonable accommodations.

Partner with experts in CEE, Financial Empowerment, to increase Schedule A hiring at CFPB.

REPORT OF ACCOMPLISHMENTS and MODIFICATIONS TO OBJECTIVE

CFPB held training sessions entitled "Human Resource Guide to American With Disabilities Act (ADA) Workplace" facilitated by the National Employment Law Institute, Director of ADA and EEO, David K. Fram, Esq.; Schedule A Information and Disability etiquette available on intranet and circulated to employees.

10. Special program plan for the recruitment, hiring, and advancement of individuals with disabilities

TABLE 35: CHANGES IN DISABLED WORKFORCE

	# on 9/30/2012	% on 9/30/2012	# on 9/30/2013	% on 9/30/2013	Net Change #	Net Change %
Total workforce	988	100%	1343	100%	355	35.93%
Reportable disability	83	8.49%	107	7.97%	24	28.92%
Targeted disability	6	0.61%	9	0.67%	3	50%

TABLE 36: APPLICATIONS AND SELECTIONS OF PERSONS WITH TARGETED DISABILITIES

Total number of applications from persons with targeted disabilities during the reporting period	910
Total number of selections of individuals with targeted disabilities during the reporting period	6

TABLE 37: OTHER EMPLOYMENT PERSONNEL PROGRAMS

	TOTAL	Reportable Disability		Targeted Disability		Not Identified		No Disability	
		#	%	#	%	#	%	#	%
Competitive promotions	N/A	N/A	N/A	N/A	N/A	N/A	N/A	N/A	N/A
Non-competitive promotions	178	24	13.48%	2	1.12%	6	3.37%	148	83.14%
Employee career development programs	No data available								
Grades 5-12	222	24	10.61%	2	0.9%	4	1.8%	194	87.39%
Grades 13-14	372	36	9.68%	3	0.81%	4	1.08%	332	89.25%
Grades 15/SES	257	20	7.78%	0	0.00%	9	3.5%	228	88.72%
Employee recognition and awards	849	80	9.42%	5	0.58%	16	1.88%	753	88.69%
Time-off awards (total hrs awarded)	No data available								
Cash awards (total $$$ awarded)	N/A	N/A	N/A	N/A	N/A	N/A	N/A	N/A	N/A
Quality-step increase	No data available								

Identification and elimination of barriers – see part I-7

Goals for targeted disabilities - CFPB has established a goal to reach 2.0% representation in the total workforce for persons with targeted disabilities by the end of FY 2015.

www.ingramcontent.com/pod-product-compliance
Lightning Source LLC
Chambersburg PA
CBHW080305180526
45167CB00006B/2674